EXPRESSIONS OF CAMEROON ART

The Franklin Collection

Tamara Northern

With contributions by Valerie Franklin, Suzanne Muchnic, Jill Salmons

*To Ruth, and the late Harry Franklin
whose search for meaning in beauty preceeded us.*

This catalogue and accompanying exhibition were
presented at:

The Los Angeles County Museum of Natural History
Los Angeles, California

Baltimore Museum of Art
Baltimore, Maryland

Hood Museum of Art
Dartmouth College
Hanover, New Hampshire

Heartfelt thanks to Honor Vandeveer

ISBN 0-9617169-0-8
Library of Congress Catalogue Card Number 86-61839
© 1986 Rembrandt Press. All rights reserved

Designed by Raess Design
Printed by The Castle Press

The unusual opportunity to participate in matters of historical significance is a special event in the lifetime of a serious collector, and as a consequence, we began looking more intensely at our own Cameroon sculpture as well as others. This led to the decision to collect in depth and breadth. In the collection are representative examples of most of the major mask types from the Grassfields, as well as stools, bowls, drinking horns, cast brass necklaces, and extraordinary figures. Also included are masks and figures from the Keaka people.

It is a lasting joy to remember our shared experiences of hopes, risks, rewards and the ultimate sense of genuine satisfaction in forming this collection. It was thrilling to find and select just the right sculpture to add to the aesthetic grouping we hoped would someday be an important resource for scholarly endeavors. In the meantime, we would be fortunate to live with these objects and preserve them for the future–a happy arrangement.

For seven years Professor Northern has been researching our collection in relationship to her overall work with the art and culture of the Cameroon. It has been stimulating for me to be on the intellectual frontiers of Cameroon studies with Professor Northern and I understand that for her, when she first discovered our material, it was like a miner finding a rich vein. Professor Northern began developing the Smithsonian Institution Traveling Exhibition Service (SITES), *The Art of the Cameroon* exhibition, and asked me to lend extensively from my collection to that show which eventually traveled for two and a half years. Upon those pieces being returned to Los Angeles, where there had been no showing of the SITES exhibit, the idea evolved to exhibit my complete collection, which would be seen for the first time in its entirety. The task was then before us, to expand on the previous Cameroon work within the framework of one person's collection, a personal selection of objects, albeit extensive in breadth and depth. We are grateful to Professor Northern for sharing with us and the public her wealth of knowledge garnered through field experience and close associations in Cameroon and intensive research in Europe as well as in America. Her brilliant mind creates reflections in the art, of a place and time past, brought forward into our world and sphere of understanding.

The richness and depth of these sculptures have provided us endless hours of fascination with the imagination and skill of the Cameroon artist. The cultural rhythms which form the matrix of Cameroon life have become meaningful through Professor Northern's scholarship. The depths of iconography and its cultural meaning to the life of the Cameroon people becomes accessible.

We have seized an opportunity that so often goes unrecognized to embark on an aesthetic adventure, not knowing where it will lead. Through love and commitment we have allowed and encouraged it to evolve to a point where others are intensely interested in learning and partaking of what this art has to offer. This exhibition and catalogue are the culmination of a lifelong interest in Cameroon art.

It is my pleasure to share my collection with you, to share the beauty, to share the power and for all of us to share the artistic manifestation of the traditional culture of the Cameroon. Each of us is made richer through understanding other peoples and other cultures, other approaches to the human existence and to different ways of success, albeit more ancient ways than ours, ways that are fascinating, genuine, and provide a reflection of mankind's past.

Valerie Franklin

9

Cameroon Grassfields and Southeastern Nigeria

Designated are relevant Grassfields kingdoms
and tribal groups on the periphery

LEGEND:

--- · --- International Boundaries

English Speaking Area

French Speaking Area

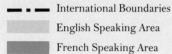

N
↑

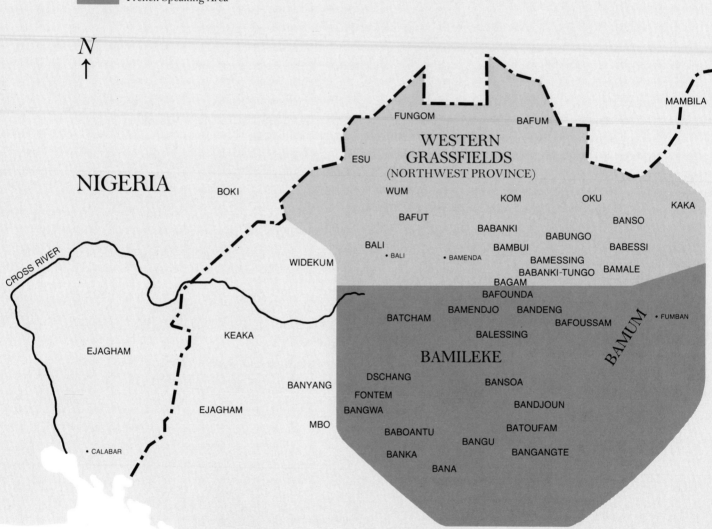

MAMBILA

NIGERIA

FUNGOM   BAFUM

ESU

WESTERN GRASSFIELDS
(NORTHWEST PROVINCE)

BOKI

WUM   KOM   OKU   KAKA

BAFUT   BANSO

BABANKI   BABUNGO

BALI   BAMBUI   BABESSI

WIDEKUM   • BALI   • BAMENDA   BAMESSING

BABANKI-TUNGO   BAMALE

BAGAM

BAFOUNDA

BAMENDJO   BANDENG

BATCHAM   BAFOUSSAM   • FUMBAN

BALESSING

TIKAR

KEAKA

BAMUM

BAMILEKE

EJAGHAM

BANYANG   DSCHANG   BANSOA

FONTEM

BANGWA   BANDJOUN

EJAGHAM

MBO   BATOUFAM

BABOANTU   BANGU

• CALABAR   BANKA   BANGANGTE

BANA

CROSS RIVER

CAMEROON

BIGHT OF BIAFRA   • DOUALA

10°

The Artistic Tradition of the Cameroon Grassfields

The art of Cameroon is a legacy of rich and diverse cultural traditions found within the boundaries of the present nation. As all African art, Cameroon art is closely linked to the historic and social contexts of its diverse populations.

Cameroon's major artistic traditions originate in the area of the Grassfields. Grassfields art has its roots in cultural systems in which kings (Fons) and their governments, interacting with the men's regulatory society (Kwifoyn), guide and guard the well-being of their people. As such, Grassfields art is primarily an art of royalty, status and wealth. Its dominant themes of royal authority and social prestige are carried out in a profusion of symbolic forms.

Grassfields art testifies to the vitality, creativity and accomplished skills of its makers. Its versatility is characterized by bold dimensions of size and visual concept rendered in styles ranging from uninhibited dynamism and impulsive exuberance to static repose and serenity. It is an art that elicits strong responses from Cameroonians and Westerners alike.

1
Janus Faced Male Mask
Western Grassfields: unspecified
wood
51 cm high
19th Century
ex-collection: Arthur Speyer

The multiple buffalo icons of the mask's
headdress connote royal power and
the Janus imagery may recall the Fon's
ability to see on all sides — to be com-
pletely informed. Together these
images constitute a "strong," very
important mask which is only once
represented in a lineage mask group.

2
Male Mask
Eastern Grassfields Periphery,
  Tikar people: Bankim kingdom
wood with raffia base
65 cm high
19th Century
ex-collection: Arthur Speyer

The Tikar masking tradition is less
prominent and diversified than that
of the Grassfields kingdoms. Pairs of
male and female masks dance at death
celebrations and at an annual harvest
dance in praise of ancestors. This male
mask with a prestige cap symbolizes
the founding ancestor of the royal
lineage.

13

The Art of Wood Carving in the Cameroon Grassfields

All Grassfields kingdoms practiced the art of wood carving. Carving was and is considered a respected, honorable, creative and lucrative skill that Fons themselves have cultivated. Most palaces had, at least intermittently, a sculptor in residence who fulfilled the needs of the palace and the regulatory society and who trained apprentices while being maintained by the Fon.

A sculptor carved for the Fon, who was his patron. His workshop was in or close to the palace precinct, and he supplied prestige sculpture for the palace and the regulatory society as well as for the kingdom's title-holders, who had to pay the Fon a fee for his carver's services. Prestige sculpture was carved upon specific requests from specific clients, mostly from within the kingdom and occasionally from without. It was not made for stock and sold or traded randomly.

14

Iconography

Grassfields culture, as part of an overarching Black African culture pattern, partakes of a fundamental and pervasive mode to express levels of human experience in iconic form. Iconic expression permits the bonding of collective and subjective levels and spheres of experience into one coherent system of representation.

Iconic expression is associative rather than conceptually analytic; its interpretation depends on even-handed measures of ethnographic knowledge and a disposition to follow and emulate the associative process by "seeing." Such interpretation may reveal what lies hidden behind cultural metaphors while also recognizing the autonomous integrity of visual representations.

The art of the Grassfields is characterized by a repertoire of human and animal icons that symbolize the values and beliefs of its cultural relief.

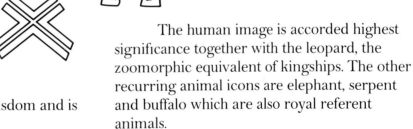

The spider is a symbol of wisdom and is used for prophecy.

The human image is accorded highest significance together with the leopard, the zoomorphic equivalent of kingships. The other recurring animal icons are elephant, serpent and buffalo which are also royal referent animals.

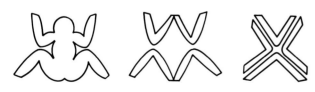

The frog symbolizes fertility and is considered a good omen.

3
**Anthropomorphic/Zoomorphic
Male Figure**
Probably Southwestern Forest:
     possibly Mbo people
wood
47 cm high
19th Century
Collected by Hans Glauning before 1908
ex-collection: Arthur Speyer

This striking sculpture shows affinities
to the figural style of the western
Bamileke people. Its admixture of
animal/spirit traits seems to consolidate
supernatural references. But its meaning and function remain elusive.

Human Figures

Carved human figures – frequently paired as male and female – are a characteristic feature of Grassfields art. Such figures represent royal memorial figures or those of important family (lineage) heads and title-holders, as well as loyal retainers of the king.

Royal memorial figures include representations of Fons, their titled wives, and queen mothers. These statues typically display the regalia of Fonship and serve as an historic record of the dynastic succession. They are among the paramount symbols of kingship and as such are displayed in the presence of the Fon during the kingdom's most important ceremonies and rites.

All memorial figures are symbols of the prevailing hierarchic social order and an affirmation of the dominant cultural values of kingship, female reproductive and productive capacities (female figures), and loyalty to the Fon (retainer figures).

4
Royal Memorial Ancestor Figure
Grassfields: unspecified
wood, camwood powder, iron,
    African civet skin
175 cm high
19th to 20th Century

This tall lean figure vested with headdress, drinking horn, cache-sexe of
civet skin and iron necklaces recalls
the regal demeanor of a royal ancestor.

Heavy traces of red camwood powder,
a substance used to indicate excep-
tional status of people and things,
attest to its function as a cult figure.
The standard prestige cap of such
figures is here rendered as a headdress with a lizard on either side, while
retaining the typical form of the bi-
tufted prestige cap. The iron accoutrements include pendants of a double
and single gong, emblem of the palace
related regulatory society (Kwifoyn).
All of these attributes, led by the significant civet skin, related in symbolic
quality to the powerful leopard pelt,
make a cohesive statement about
Fonship.

The sole reliance on criteria of iconography and style — in the absence of
collecting documentation — leaves
more specific provenance attribution
equivocal: however, the rigid frontality
and static posture of this statue seem
to relegate it to the Western Grassfields.

5
Male Figure
Grassfields: Bamileke people
wood, camwood powder
38 cm high
19th Century

This figure may depict a retainer, wearing a prestige cap and displaying the gesture of deference (hand covering the mouth — here rendered with iconographic license as hand touching the beard), while speaking with the Fon.

Fig. 7   Fig. 6

(See color plate on page 22)

6
Memorial Figure of a Royal Titled Wife
Grassfields: Bamileke people,
    Bangwa kingdom
wood
82 cm high
19th century

This figure claims an illustrious collecting history. It was collected among the Bangwa between 1897 and 1898 by Gustav Conrau, who was a German merchant-explorer and colonial agent and was the first white man to reach the Bangwa kingdoms in 1897. His primary mission was to recruit Grassfields men for German plantation labor at the coast. He also collected extensively en route during two sojourns among the Bangwa. His longest stay, as a captive, was in Fontem, the largest of the Bangwa kingdoms. It seems probable that this sculpture originated in Fontem, but Conrau's collecting activities in the smaller kingdoms around Fontem make this less than a certainty. Conrau died in Fontem in early 1899 under duress and probably by his own hand.

This figure is one of the first major Grassfields sculptures to have been collected and to convey to a surprised but appreciative circle of German cognoscenti the sophistication of Grassfields art. It entered the holdings of the then Konigliches Museum für Völkerkunde, Berlin, as part of the Conrau collection (III C10529) and was later, in the early 1930's acquired by Arthur Speyer, noted Berlin collector

and German pendant to the dean of African art collectors, Charles Ratton, who shared subsequent temporary ownership of this coveted sculpture before passing it on to the Princess Gourielli (Helena Rubinstein), whose magnificent collection of African art was formed in the 1930's. It remained in the Rubinstein collection as one of its outstanding works of art for nearly three decades, when it was acquired by the Franklin family from the Rubinstein estate through auction (Parke-Bernet) in 1966.

Known in popular conception as the Bangwa Queen Figure because of her regal demeanor, this figure represents a woman in her dual role as priestess of the earth cult and mother of twins. She is shown in the act of dancing and singing the song of the earth as she would at the funeral celebration for a deceased king.

Among the Bangwa, as in other Grassfields kingdoms, parents of twins are conceived of as having a special and close association with fertility (by patent analogy) and the life-giving and renewing forces of the earth. Accordingly, some twin parents gain elevated and important status as diviners and guardians of the earth. This figure is marked by the valued attributes of full sexual and social maturity and carries the basketry rattle of the leader in the dance of the earth, while also displaying the typical accoutrements of royal status: collars of glass beads, a necklace of carved leopard teeth pendants, beaded loin string, and ivory armlets and anklets.

Iconography, while consistent about salient symbols, can at the same time be selective subject to the individual artist's discretion as long as local iconographic and aesthetic canons are not violated. Departures from the norm — or what we would consider as such based on our knowledge — do occur. It is furthermore worth restating that our knowledge, gained nearly a century after the full-blown context of this art and from informants equally long removed from it (at least in time, if not in cultural perception) remains fragmentary. We know only pieces of the mosaic and attempt to join them meaningfully.

Robert Brain, an anthropologist, worked among the Bangwa in the 1960's, and his interpretation of this figure as a mother of twins is an example of this dilemma. His field observations established unequivocally that cowrie shells are the attributes of twin mothers among the Bangwa. Yet this figure is missing the telling cowrie shells. Were it not for collector Conrau's skeletal information of the figure's name being *njuindem/ngwindem*, meaning, "woman of God," according to Brain, and Brain's own field observations of an actual *ngwindem* at work, his attribution of this figure to the context of twin mothers/earth guardians would not have been possible. Yet one might still argue that because the important iconographic indicator of cowrie shells is absent, this figure may not be a representation of a twin mother, but of a royal titled wife or princess (notice the exclusive royal anklets) with outstanding abilities as a diviner concurring with her role as "woman of God." This assignation would be entirely in keeping with the multi-valent quality of symbolic representations and would reaffirm the figure's long standing popular designation as "Queen."

This figure of a woman in the bloom of life, implying the promise of generating life in abundance, is one of the most acclaimed and admired sculptures of African art. Eckart von Sydow, German art historian and one of the earliest scholars of non-western art history, singled out this figure as the rare exception from the general canon of static frontality common to much of ethnographic art and as the most powerful example of the art of Cameroon. Although he wrote in 1930 at a time when the corpus of African art known to us was more limited than it is now, subsequent accolades have been no less laudatory, and William Fagg, writing three decades later, declares "This celebrated figure of a dancing woman bids fair to be the finest expression of movement in all African sculpture."

7
Royal Memorial Ancestor Figure
Grassfields: Bamileke people,
  Bangwa kingdom
wood
89 cm high
19th Century

This figure has generally been re-
garded as the male partner of the
Bangwa Queen Figure. Its aesthetic
realization leaves no doubt that both
were carved by the same artist, whose
individual hand is apparent in the
stylistic rendering of both figures. While
they exemplify a Bangwa (and perhaps
a Fontem) style, they also carry the
signature — as it were — of one carver.
This in itself, however, does not es-
tablish or confirm the figures as a pair.

This male figure was also collected by
Conrau among the Bangwa in 1897-98
and was deposited in the Museum für
Völkerkunde, Berlin, (III C10518) where
it remained until 1926, when it was ob-
tained by collector Arthur Speyer, who
in turn offered it to the Franklin family
after their acquisition of the female
dancing figure, in order to reconstitute
the pair.

The regalia seen on this figure — the
prestige cap, collar of beads, necklace
of carved leopard teeth, ivory armlets,
leopard-skin anklets and calabash —
are those reserved to kings and typically characterize royal memorial ancestor figures. In the possible pair
context, the female dancing figure
would be confirmed as a titled royal
wife or princess. Both figures exemplify
the vibrant and exuberant expressive
quality for which much of Bamileke art
is known and lauded.

(See color plate on page 23)

8
**Memorial figure of a Royal Titled Wife
with Child**
Grassfields: Bamileke people
wood
74 cm high
19th Century
ex-collection: Arthur Speyer

The male prestige cap, necklace of
large valuable chevron beads, armlets
and anklets identify this woman as a
royal titled wife. She also symbolizes
maternity: her saturated vital female
body promises more children, and her
gesture of cradling the infant's head
expresses nurture, care and affection.

The Bangwa Queen as Documented by Man Ray

Man Ray (1890–1977) was a legendary artist, better known for his wit and irreverent philosophy than for his artwork. He was, however, a prodigious creator of photographs, films, paintings and assemblages of found objects.

He was born in Philadephia and studied painting in New York. His friendship with Alfred Stieglitz inspired his interest in photography, which he took up in 1915. He met Marcel Duchamp the same year and, in 1917, collaborated with him and Francis Picabia in founding the New York Dada movement. Man Ray went to Paris in 1921, where he joined the European Dada group and later the Surrealists. The Nazi occupation of Paris forced his return to the United States in 1940. He stayed after World War II had ended, settling in Hollywood and finally returning to Paris in 1950.

Man Ray's sculptural "objects" such as "Le Cadeau," an iron with sharp tacks protruding from its flat surface, epitomize the Dadaists' flair for absurdity and their preference for unorthodox materials. "Observation Time–The Lovers," his painting of gigantic lips floating in a sky above the Griffith Park Observatory in Los Angeles, epitomizes the Surrealists' propensity for a-logical juxtapositions in a dream-world reality.

Considered one of the most important photographers of his era, Man Ray pioneered the artistic exploration of "rayographs" (images made without a camera by placing objects on photosensitive paper and exposing them to light) in the 1920s. During the following decade, he developed techniques of solarization (the reversal of dark and light tones through overexposure).

In close contact with the creative communities of Los Angeles and Paris, Man Ray photographed many celebrities, as well as his wife, Juliette, and other models. He often drew relationships between his sitters and objects posed with them or transformed his subjects with costumes and technical manipulations. His interest in primitive art, seen in several photographs, echoed that of Picasso and other modernists.

In this relatively straight photograph of a nude and possibly pregnant model with the Bangwa Queen (probably taken in Paris in the 1930s), Man Ray developed dual themes of diversity and continuity. Contrasting a living light-skinned woman with a vigorous representation of a black female, he unified the two in an arabesque composition. The pair are physically entwined in a rhythmic flow of arcs and oval shapes even as they present us with a striking comparison.

Suzanne Muchnic

Mambila Figures

On the northern periphery of the Grassfields extending into Nigeria in the west live the Mambila. They are an agricultural people living in autonomous villages of egalitarian lineage organization. Although Mambila art has long been acknowledged as one of the distinct and significant sculpture styles of Cameroon, our knowledge of its history and iconographic evolution has remained superficial.

Much of Mambila art – carved by male artists – is associated with the seasonal cycles of planting and harvesting and the cult of ancestors whose material abode is the guarded shrine of every family compound.

Fig. 9

9

Pair of Male and Female Ancestor Figures

Northern Plateau area: Mambila people
wood, kaolin, camwood powder
37 cm high
19th to 20th Century

These small but sturdy figures carved in typical Mambila fashion charm the viewer with details of features and adornment delineated in red and white pigment on a black background. The high peaked cap on the male figure is echoed sculpturally by the triangles created by the pointed face and the hands held to the chin. The female figure is more rounded, a slightly less stark version of the Mambila aesthetic.

10

Male Ancestor Figure

Northern Plateau area: Mambila people
wood
48 cm high
19th to early 20th Century

Mambila sculpture at its best expresses intensity and controlled force. This figure is one such example and illustrates the recurrent features of Mambila figures: a heart-shaped face, detailed with small wooden pegs outlining its delicate shape, and the spring-like contained energy about to be released throughout by the rhythmically bent arms and legs. Ancestor figures as receptacles for ancestral spirits controlled the welfare of the living, who depended on the good will of the ancestors for health, fertility, good harvest, luck in hunting and fishing and success in trade — in short, their material well being.

Stools and Prestige Objects

The center of the kingdom's art is the palace. The royal treasury comprises the full and splendid array of insignia that represent royal status and prestige. From the architecture itself to the drinking horns, pipes, ivory trumpets, jewelry and food vessels, palace art proclaims the wealth and vitality of the Fon and kingdom.

Prestige objects are worn and used by the Fon and, with his consent, also by select high-ranking title-holders. These insignia are the visual validation of high status, and they are distinct in their materials and symbolic imagery from common utilitarian objects.

The stool is the foremost prestige object as symbol of royal office. The act of sitting represents the Fon's confidence and command sanctioned by tradition and his direct link to the royal ancestors, his predecessors on the throne. Coupled with royal icons used as caryatids, the stool explicitly upholds the Fon's authority.

A Fon owns a number of stools: some are inherited from predecessors and are honored as memorials; some are carved during his lifetime. There is usually one specific stool that symbolizes his office. This stool or throne would be his seat during audiences with his subjects, at public ceremonies or during formal receptions for visiting Fons and dignitaries.

11
Prestige Stool
Western Grassfields:
  Babanki-Tungo style
wood
34 cm high
19th Century

Similar iconography to Fig. 13, however, this one has two rows of heads on wavy bands.

Fig. 12

Fig. 13

Fig. 14

12
Prestige Stool
Western Grassfields: unspecified
wood
45 cm high
19th Century

Rich in iconography, the primary
images of this stool, nude human
figures, and heads, symbolize the
human resources as strength and support of the kingdom. The spider and
frog symbols on the supporting pillars
respectively connote wisdom and
fertility. It may have belonged to the
palace or to a high-ranking title-holder.

13
Prestige Stool
Western Grassfields: Babanki style
wood
48 cm high
19th Century

Three rows of multiple male heads with
prestige caps are represented on wavy
bands. Although the bands are seemingly sculptural devices to anchor the
heads, they can also be interpreted as
frog signs.

14
Prestige Stool
Western Grassfields: Babanki style
wood
28 cm high
19th Century

Male figures wearing prestige caps
and multiple armlets (of ivory) may
symbolize the kingdom's dynasty,
which legitimizes and supports the
Fon's authority. Vertical rows of cowrie
shells on short columns represent
wealth.

30

15
Prestige Chair
Grassfields: Bamum people,
  Fumban palace
wood
92 cm high
Early to mid 20th Century

This chair belongs to the genre of African "contact art" — that is, a kind of art created by native peoples in response to intensive contact with Europeans and in some measure imitative of European forms. Contact art is judged negatively by some as an acculturated art form devoid of traditional precolonial functions, while it is seen by others as an innovative response to the exposure of new visual stimuli and a new clientele for art, demonstrating peoples' adaption to change, which is as old as humankind.

In this example of contact art, the indigenous round form of the typical Grassfields prestige stool and its traditional icons have been retained. But the leopards and female retainer figure have been placed to approximate the form of a European armchair. As is frequently the case with contact art, the traditional iconic code has not been observed. Hence there are two leopards instead of the customary solitary predator, and they are associated with the female figure, despite the fact that women cannot appropriate leopards in the kingdom of Bamum nor in any other Grassfields kingdom. The direct visual association of the female figure and the leopards is alien to the traditional iconic code.

The motif of the double-headed serpent seen at the bottom is a common theme in Bamum royal art. However, this very specific form of representation is traditionally not used as stool support, but does occur as support for royal beds. While it may seem insignificant to distinguish between a stool-chair and a bed, both furniture from our perspective, precolonial Bamum artistic canons did exercise such distinctions quite rigorously, because neither stool nor bed were only furniture.

Examples of this type of armchair now in museums and private collections appear to have been made in various parts of the Grassfields during the period of British and French colonial administration, which was of course a long one, circa 1918-1960. There is some, but less, evidence that this type of object was also produced during the preceding German colonial period. In either case, such chairs would have been made initially on commission for "important" Europeans, men of status, such as the colonial district officer and the regular trader. They were not necessarily sold, but also figured as articles of royal gift exchange, thus remaining within the traditional culture pattern, according to which a Fon honored and obliged someone of equal prestige with a gift. Eventually, as cash currency became more common and necessary in daily economic transactions, they became articles for sale.

The pan-African tourist art phenomenon that developed in response to the post 1950's tourist boom finally accounts for such armchairs to be made and sold as tourist art. But as tourist art, their quality is generally inferior: their carving is crude, the images a hapless assortment of disparate iconic motifs, and the surface is frequently characterized by facile pyro accents. This genre also includes "tables" in oversize format of the traditional round stool. However, such armchairs are also used presently as royal chairs by contemporary Grassfields kings. The present Fon of Nso uses two such chairs made in Babungo under the supervision of the Fon of Babungo. They are prominently displayed as regalia in the reception hall and courtyard of the Nso palace. Their altered new form has gained acceptance in fulfilling an old cultural need.

16
Stool or Calabash Stand
Grassfields: Bamileke people
wood
41 cm high
19th Century

The expressive figure of a monkey
displays a flexed arm and leg position
creating a sparse figural style of open
geometric volumes which is occasionally found on seated figures.

17
Prestige Calabash Stand
Western Grassfields: northwestern
    perimeter: Esu, Fungom or Bafum
    kingdoms
wood
29 cm high
19th Century

The caryatids here exemplify the
distinct figural style of these northern
kingdoms: compressed triangular face
punctuated by eyes, nose and mouth,
and a body rendered in dramatic
stylization.

18
Prestige Pipe Bowl
Grassfields: Bamileke people,
  Bangangte kingdom
Terra cotta
14 cm high
19th Century

Pipe bowls in figural form from the Cameroon Grassfields are often compelling small sculptures. This example represents a seated male figure with prestige cap, probably a Fon. Typically, the well-articulated head predominates proportionately over the compacted mass of body and limbs.

Prestige pipes of terra cotta (as distinct from common utilitarian pipes) were characterized by a complex imagery of human and animal icons. As regalia of Fons and title-holders, they were indispensable personal prestige items, cared for and carried after their owners by retainers, and displayed as status indicators on ceremonial occasions.

19
Trumpet
Grassfields: unspecified
ivory, lizard skin (indigenous repair with
  raffia lashing)
56 cm high
19th Century

Ivory trumpets are owned exclusively by the palace. Their deep mellow calls resound around the palace at state events and herald the Fon's passage through his village on formal occasions. As prized regalia they are kept in the care of palace retainers.

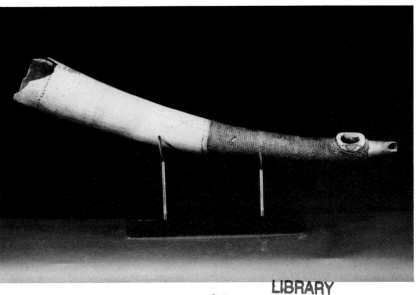

33

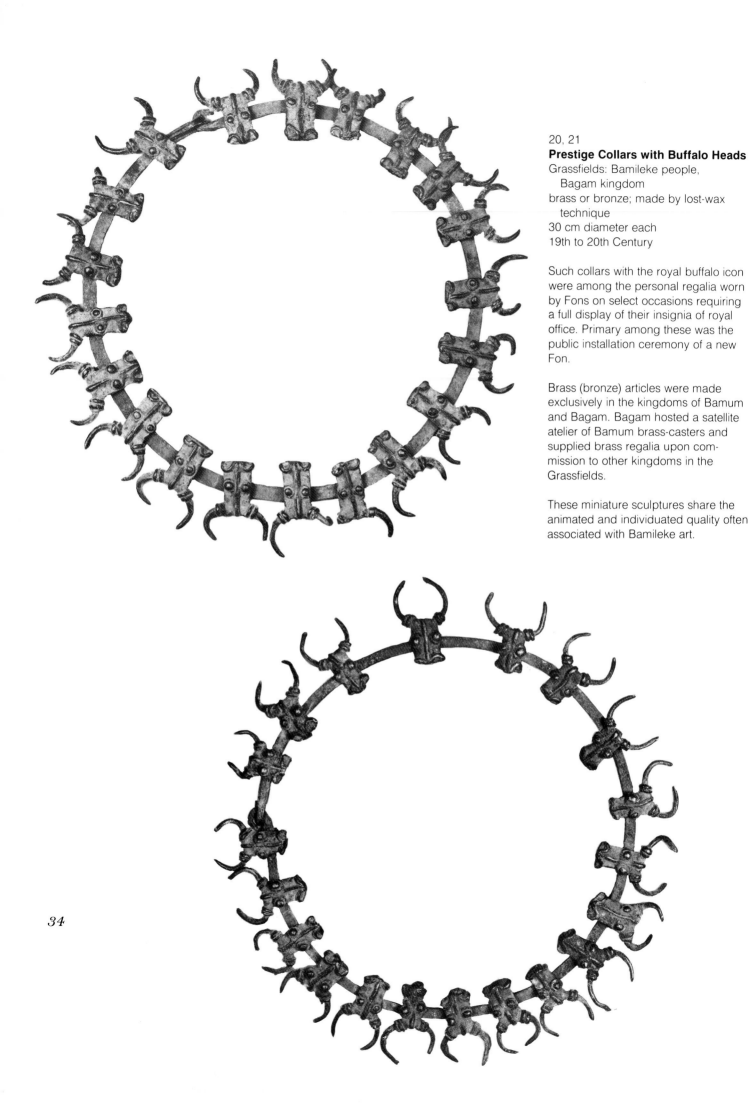

20, 21
Prestige Collars with Buffalo Heads
Grassfields: Bamileke people,
    Bagam kingdom
brass or bronze; made by lost-wax
    technique
30 cm diameter each
19th to 20th Century

Such collars with the royal buffalo icon
were among the personal regalia worn
by Fons on select occasions requiring
a full display of their insignia of royal
office. Primary among these was the
public installation ceremony of a new
Fon.

Brass (bronze) articles were made
exclusively in the kingdoms of Bamum
and Bagam. Bagam hosted a satellite
atelier of Bamum brass-casters and
supplied brass regalia upon commission to other kingdoms in the
Grassfields.

These miniature sculptures share the
animated and individuated quality often
associated with Bamileke art.

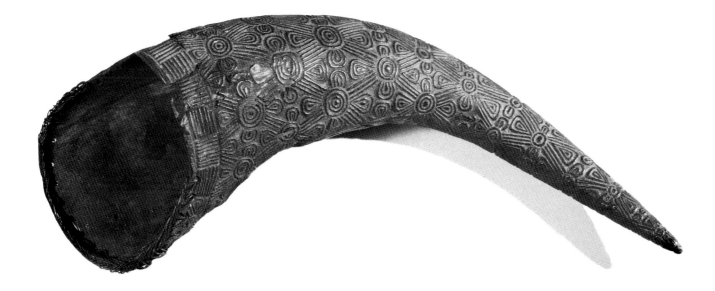

22
Prestige Drinking Horn
Grassfields: Bamum kingdom
Buffalo horn, brass
42 cm high
19th Century

Imagery of interlocking schematized
spiders.

Drinking horns from Bamum are distinct in that the entire horn surface is
carved, while those from other Grassfields kingdoms are commonly carved
in patterned center sections, leaving a
plain area on both extremes of the horn.

23
Prestige Drinking Horn
Western Grassfields: unspecified
cow horn
21 cm high
19th to 20th Century

Imagery of two male faces with
prestige caps and several versions
of the frog.

In all Grassfields kingdoms, drinking
horns, plain or ornate, are a man's
most important personal article, a
reference to the significance of palm
wine for shared sociability and pleasure
and as a sacrificial libation substance.
Delicately carved with royal symbols,
drinking horns such as these are part
of a Fon's and title-holder's treasured
regalia. The horns may be made of
buffalo, dwarf cattle, ram or cow horn.
Buffalo and dwarf cattle horns were
widely reserved for palace use, because of the animals' symbolic and
economic importance for the palace.

24
Prestige Bowl
Western Grassfields: unspecified
wood
30 cm high
19th Century

This ceremonial food bowl is carved
with two of the most prominent
icons: frogs with ornamental doubling
of the head around the bowl and
spiders around the base.

36

25
Prestige Bowl
Western Grassfields:
    northwestern perimeter
wood
30 cm high
19th to 20th Century

This bowl was used to hold kola nuts
for the Fon and palace guests. Its
stand represents the frog motif as
symbol of fertility.

26, 27
Prestige Bowls
Grassfields: Eastern Bamileke people
   or Bamum kingdom
wood
24 cm high; 28 cm high
19th Century

These food bowls are supported by a
leopard in typical crouching stance.
Food would have been prepared by
royal women and served in these
bowls to the king and attending
dignitaries. Ornate basketry lids or
mats of woven raffia fiber covered the
food on such occasions.

The Iron Technology in the Cameroon Grassfields

Babungo is a kingdom with a population of circa 15,000 people located in the Ndop plain of the Grassfields on an old, well-traveled trade route, now the major artery traversing the Grassfields. Hoe cultivation is the basis for subsistence economy, as is the case for all of the Grassfields kingdoms. However, Babungo is also the most important iron-working center in the Grassfields. Slag-heaps approximating 15 feet in height are evidence of the antiquity and continuity of its iron technology tradition. For at least the past two centuries Babungo has occupied a place of importance and influence among kingdoms of the Grassfields due to its position as supplier of iron implements.

The chain of mountains to the north of Babungo was once rich in the ferrous surface ore deposits which constituted the basis for the area's iron technology until gradual depletion of the deposits in the 1920's. For the next three decades, blacksmithing depended on the use of slag for its iron content and on European import iron until the latter became the primary source of iron raw material in the 1950's.

Traditionally, although not consistently, smelting, blacksmithing and charcoal-making have been specialized skills in Babungo. Smelters and smiths both traded for charcoal, while smiths also traded for bloom. Two furnace types of the African smelting technology have been successively used in Babungo: the Catalan type, an open fire in a banked depression in the ground, and the Mediterranean type, a domed clay roasting furnace.

The Finkwi Quarter of Babungo is home to the blacksmiths. It is the largest quarter and, unlike other quarters, still retains houses of the traditional Grassfields type. Blacksmiths are reputed to keep more tenaciously to old customs than other villagers. In the late 1970's, Finkwi counted 48 active blacksmiths' compounds, with a forge to each compound.

The production team of a forge usually consists of the master blacksmith, who is the compound head, and a number of his adult sons. Intermittent help is provided by male children – frequently at the bellows – and wives, who bring food directly to the forge during days of intensive work. Adult male lineage members who are skilled in smithing, but who do not own their own smithy, substitute occasionally for a son. Every forge specializes in the manufacture of one type of implement: knives, cutlasses, swords, spear and arrow points, hoes, or ritual paraphernalia such as gongs and staffs. There is even further specialization as to the form or style of a given artefact. Swords with a crescent-shaped point are made by one blacksmith, while others specialize in the three other standard types of swords. These artefacts, formerly traded but now sold, find a wide distribution through the markets of the Grassfields. Certain articles, such as ritual paraphernalia and ceremonial swords, are made on a commission basis and are not publicly bartered or sold.

Tih Ndula Bobo of Finkwi Quarter, Babungo – commonly known as Pa Tih – is a master blacksmith. He has two wives and sixteen children. His second son, Kometa, now about twenty-five years old, has been apprenticed as a blacksmith and will be Pa Tih's successor at the forge. The Tih smithy, located on the periphery of the compound, is typical in its construction, inventory of tools, and techniques of Finkwi forges. A pitched roof on a raffia pole frame with grass shingling – open on two sides – defines the work space. A flat, large, rounded stone serves as anvil; it has been in the Tih family for many generations and is an important and prized possession. Several smaller stones are used as hammers to pound the raw material – bloom cake or, presently, scrap iron parts – into the rough shape of the implement-to-be. Two iron hammers serve to flatten and smooth the metal into its desired shape with a clean, smooth surface and precisely delineated edges. This process of forging

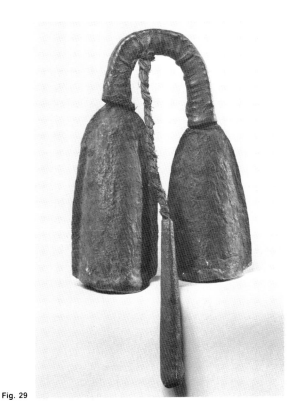

Fig. 29

28, 29
Double Gongs
Western Grassfields: unspecified
iron, raffia, hide
64 cm high; 31 cm high
19th to 20th Century

Double gongs, joined by a handle and commonly made of iron, are the visual emblem and authoritative voice of the regulatory society and are played at the secret meetings of its exclusively male membership. Gongs such as these were made on commission by blacksmiths in several specialized iron production centers — notably those of the Ndop plain, led by Babungo — and were disseminated for use in kingdoms over major parts of the Grassfields. The blacksmiths of Babungo are still presently the main suppliers of gongs.

Fig. 28

depends on reheating the iron intermittently to keep it malleable. Reheating is done on the open fire-place, where charcoal is kept glowing by air infusion blasts from the bellows (the air is conducted through two clay tubes, *tuyères,* lightly covered with soil). To use a stone as anvil has an advantage, in that there is less heat loss of the iron than is the case with European steel anvils, which absorb heat rapidly. Consequently, the metal remains malleable longer, reheating is less frequent, and the work process improves in efficiency. The last step in finishing an implement is polishing. Traditionally done with natural abrasive materials, such as fine sand, this lengthy process is

rarely applied now. Instead, metal files are generally used, but they do not achieve the same smooth surface and tend to leave visible marks. The presence or absence of file marks on an implement can be a criterion for determining whether it was manufactured recently or in the traditional way.

In Finkwi the technique of blacksmithing, as practiced by Pa Tih, has so far remained essentially unchanged over the centuries. Artefacts which demonstrate functional efficiency and aesthetic quality, made by a pre-industrial technology, are still characteristic of Babungo iron-working.

39

30
Drum
Western Grassfields; Bali?
wood, hide, raffia bast cord
110 cm high
19th to 20th Century

Drums are indispensable in any African
musical performance, for the drumbeat
provides the complex rhythmic structure so dominant in African music.
Based on its imagery, this drum belonged either to the regulatory society
(Kwifoyn) or the palace. This imagery
can be read as double gongs (of iron),
the principal emblem of the regulatory
society; human heads and alternating
female and male figures (with drinking
horn) as representing the human resources of lineages; spears as symbols
of defense and prowess in hunting and
war; spiders (at base) as the pervasive
symbol of ancestral wisdom and
prophecy.

The Blacksmiths Story from Babungo

A verbatim interview with Father Foambi, ritual head of the blacksmiths, by Ntshuo Emmanuel Mbute of Babungo in April 1974.

N: *I have come to hear from you the story of the blacksmiths. I heard that your father (forefather) descended from heaven with a sledge-hammer. Can you tell me how it happened? Maybe you heard the same as I heard because it happened a long time ago when we were not yet born, tell me how it happened.*

F: Well, it is so that my father came from heaven. I only heard it and did not see it. He came with a hammer in his hand to be forging with, and the father of my mother, the man whose compound my mother came from, he is the man who brought the bellow. He came and joined my father. He was blowing the bellow and my father took the hammer and was forging with. The forge was owned by them, the two of them.

N: *Where was he forging?*

F: He was forging just in his compound.

N: *Is the forge still in his compound now?*

F: Yes, it is still there.

N: *The sledge, your father brought, where is it?*

F: All the hammers are still in my compound.

N: *Can people still take it and be forging with?*

F: That special sledge is just half now, it is broken. Because it is a thing which cannot get finish. They cannot be forging with, but they take a sample and make new hammers to replace the other one, as a lawful thing.

N: *Is it kept where they used to be forging?*

F: That one is kept in the house.

N: *Where is the old forge?*

F: It is in my compound. [But temporarily fallen into disuse.]

N: *Why can they not rebuild it and be forging there?*

F: Well, it shall be rebuilt because my son has learned blacksmith, so I shall rebuild it. He will try to enter the forge again because I cannot lack a forge.

N: *It is good, that you let your children rebuild it because it is where forging came from.*

F: It is the same place where that sledge-hammer is kept and it happens that if anyone says anything wrong, and we take the hammer and it into a pot of oil, and if he drinks he will not stay alive. If we swear something and take the sledge-hammer which my father brought from its place and put it into palm-wine and if he drinks he will never stay on earth, with this thing in your stomach, you will never stay alive. This is the reason why we keep that special hammer aside, because it is our bad place where this hammer is.

N: *As your father brought the forging, what is your benefit now?*

F: Our benefit from the forge is that all people are forging now so that no one of our quarter men has to suffer again. Unless he has not an interest in forging, because we do not have another trade than forging.

N: *Do people pay a sort of tribute to you?*

F: People don't pay tribute to me because my father came and taught everybody. It is only that, if there is any forging business, I shall be the man ahead.

N: *Thank you!*

Literal transcription from Babungo into English by Ntshuo E. Mbute and Willi and Vreni Schaub, Summer Institute of Linguistics, Babungo.

Blacksmiths in the Cultural Matrix

Blacksmiths throughout Black Africa have occupied an ambiguous and enigmatic social position. Very frequently they constitute an ethnic entity different from the main population of farmers in a given ethnic group. As is the case for Babungo, local oral histories commonly refer to smiths as the first inhabitants of a given settled area, while the presence of the larger part of the population is ascribed to later immigrations. This separate ethnic identity of the smiths is often manifest in traits of culture patterns which differ from the prevailing norm of the farming population and relegate the smiths to a distinctive social position within the larger social structure. Smiths as a group are feared, looked upon with awe, reverence or respect, and at times despised. Blacksmiths are different, but they are needed. The farmer and the hunter – as formerly the warrior – are dependent on them for implements, which only smiths can supply. An acute awareness of the specialized and exclusive knowledge inherent in blacksmithing skills pervades the general perception of the smiths: they are able to transform seemingly intractable matter into useful implements by the controlled use of fire. This adds yet another dimension to their difference. But beyond the awe inspired by the smiths' technical abilities, their closeness to and constant contact with the potent natural phenomena of fire and earth-matter/ore create an association with the realm of the supernatural. Legends of the supernatural origin of blacksmithing, such as the Babungo example, underscore and actualize this association and place smiths in the center of a network of forces beyond common experience.

In the language of the Babungo, two terms are used in reference to blacksmiths. *Wuu ndaa,* "person of the smithy," is the denotative term for all blacksmiths, men who exercise the skill of forging iron. The other term, *iye,* is connotative, in that it refers to the smiths as a social entity whose symbol is the hammer of supernatural origin. In the strict sense the *iye* are a group of nine men who ritually represent all smiths. But *iye* is also a distinct social category comprising all blacksmiths. As *iye* all blacksmiths are categorically barred from

Master blacksmith Pa Tih in his forge
working on the leaf-shaped half of
a gong.
T.N. 1974

titled membership in the regulatory society,
which is the executive agency of government
in the kingdom. While respected and admired
for their skills as blacksmiths, the channels of
social and political mobility open to most
Babungo men under certain conditions are
not accessible to them. Although Father
Foambi is the leader of the *iye,* for example, he
is not Quarter Head of Finkwi, which includes
more smiths than farmers in its population.
The quarter headship is a social and political
office which carries a title in the regulatory

society, and Father Foambi, therefore, cannot
occupy this office. On the other hand, when
the most feared and hence to be avoided mask
society, *jau,* passes Father Foambi's compound
on the way to a nocturnal death celebration,
the members of *jau* have to stop "talking" –
they have to behave respectfully – while passing. Should Father Foambi approach them
with his iron hammer *(loa),* they turn and
run. At death celebrations at the Palace, Father
Foambi and his eight *iye* represent the blacksmiths. They hold up their hammers and then
beat the ground, a ritual gesture which
requires compensation with a goat from the
king, an equally significant gesture.

Pa Tih, as well-respected master of his
craft and lineage head, was accorded the right
to own a mask group. But his masks had to be
different in iconography and medium from
those of the prevailing norm. They are not
carved of wood but made of an amalgam of
mostly fibrous materials. The leader mask,
danced by him, is at the extreme right, the
second leader mask at the extreme left. Both
have the mask vestment with human hair common to the dominant masking tradition. Pa
Tih is very proud of his mask group and refers
to its difference in positive terms, namely that
he has the right of objection for anyone else to
own masks of this type.

Pa Tih's mask group with drum and
xylophone in front of its secluded
storage house.
T.N. 1974

Grassfields Masks

Masks are owned by several constituencies within Grassfields kingdoms, but primarily by the regulatory society (Kwifoyn) and important lineages, and they always have to be licensed by Kwifoyn. Kwifoyn is the agency of social control and law enforcement in Grassfields kingdoms. With the Fon, it guards and maintains the social norms, civic morale and religious beliefs of the kingdom.

Kwifoyn's members are men of status and wealth who hold their meetings in secret and conduct their missions under the guise of masks or in the secrecy of the dark night. Masks are instrumental in the exercise of Kwifoyn's power by conferring anonymity upon its members under the disguise of masks. Most Grassfields masks are worn atop the head over a see-through cloth covering the wearer's face. Masking is complete with a vestment enveloping the body and with accoutrements that further identify the role of the mask. The mask face or head is the most expressive part, revealing through its imagery the symbolic associations that sanction the power of the mask.

Kwifoyn and lineage masks perform publicly at the commemorative death celebrations of Fons and title-holders and at the kingdoms' annual dance, a high point of celebration during the festive cycle of the dry season. The performance of Kwifoyn masks is a solemn occasion, while the dances of lineage mask groups, following upon Kwifoyn, also provide a dimension of entertainment.

Large and historically important lineages are accorded the privilege of owning mask groups by consent of the Fon and Kwifoyn. One such lineage mask group may contain 8–30 masks which are danced by the owner's male lineage members. The dance sequence is loosely structured but generally includes certain obligatory mask types: a male leader mask followed by female masks alternating with male and animal masks and concluding with a second leader mask, usually an animal representation. This second leader mask should represent a high-ranking animal symbol, ideally the elephant, but this practice is no longer consistently maintained.

Stars identify those masks which, on the basis of shared stylistic traits, can be attributed to one sculptor or atelier active in an as-yet-unspecified kingdom of the Grassfields.

It is to be noted that there are some variations in the membership and internal structure of the regulatory society and its relationship to the palace when one considers the entire Grassfields culture complex. But the functional aspects as outlined here remain essentially the same.

Entrance of a lineage mask group
led by leader mask, *Nkang*, at a commemorative death celebration in
kingdom of Oku.
T.N. 1976

31
*Male Mask
Western Grassfields: unspecified
wood, cowrie shells, glass beads and
   traces of camwood powder
34 cm high
20th Century

This is a typical leader mask representing a male face — indicated by the
hairdress and beard. The leader mask
— *Nkang, Nkam, Akam* — leads its
mask group into and out of the performance arena and dictates the dance
style of his group. The leader mask is
characterized by a garment with tufts of
human hair and by two staffs which
aggressively augment the mask's role
as symbol of male authority and
strength. This example was the leader
mask of a mask group owned by a
prince, as manifest by the cowrie shells
and bead accoutrements reserved for
royals.

At the end of a commemorative
death celebration in Oku, the formal
ambiance of the occasion gives way
to spirited participation by spectators. A leader mask, *Nkang*, of a lineage mask group is seen here sharing
the dancing arena with female lineage
members of the deceased. At the left
a royal wife with identifying head
circlet of white buttons, a substitute
for cowrie shells.
T.N. 1976

32
Male Mask
Western Grassfields: unspecified
wood
36 cm high
19th to 20th Century

Leader mask of a lineage mask group.

In points of morphology and type, the masks of lineage and Kwifoyn mask groups are indistinguishable when they are seen out of context. In context, Kwifoyn mask groups perform solemnly in the aura of serious conduct and attention which has been set by the powerful single Kwifoyn masks preceding them, while lineage mask groups provide an element of entertainment and virtuosity dancing for the benefit of the spectators and the gratification of the masked dancers themselves as well as the orchestra.

At present lineage mask groups are numerically large — 30 masks are not uncommon — while Kwifoyn mask groups are generally half this size. It is not clear whether lineage mask groups have always been as large, but I suspect that they have not and their present size is a consequence of the inroads of increasing secularization of this mask context. While not insurmountable — given the frailty of the human condition when facing a possible gain — it would be a difficult task to obtain (buy) a mask from a Kwifoyn mask group, considering Kwifoyn's focal role as agency of traditional government. The same does not apply in the same measure to masks of a lineage mask group. Lineage mask groups are farther removed from Kwifoyn's control and can be more subject to manipulative control by their owners. As long as a mask is eventually replaced, its sale from a lineage mask group is a minor and pardonable infraction of the rules. Hence the reasonable assumption, that most of the masks in European and American collections originated from lineage mask groups.

A variety of male masks, interspersed with a Buffalo mask can be seen dancing in the mask group Nsum from Keyone Quarter, Oku.
T.N. 1974

47

33
Male Mask
Western Grassfields: unspecified
wood
38 cm high
19th to 20th Century

Leader mask of a lineage mask group.

When masks dance, their performance
requires a minimal orchestra of drums,
xylophone and rattles.

34
Male Mask
Western Grassfields: unspecified
wood
41 cm high
19th to 20th Century

Leader mask of a lineage mask group.

35
Male Mask
Western Grassfields: northwestern
   perimeter: Bafum and Fungom
   kingdoms
wood with traces of kaolin and
   camwood powder
33 cm high
19th Century

This mask with its striated male headdress is probably the local version of
Mabu, the regulatory society's lictor
mask. It is rendered in the unique
sculptural style of the northwestern
Grassfields kingdoms.

36
Male Mask
Western Grassfields: northwestern
  perimeter: Bafum or Fungom
  kingdoms
wood with traces of kaolin and
  camwood powder
40 cm high
19th Century

This mask may also represent *Mabu*,
the local regulatory society's runner or
lictor mask. As the voice of the regulatory society, *Mabu's* tasks include
announcing official decrees in the
market. The mask would be complete
with a feather vestment and several
staffs.

37
Male Mask
Western Grassfields: Northwestern
    perimeter: Bafum or Fungom
    kingdoms
wood with traces of kaolin
26 cm high, 35 cm deep/profile

The prestige cap and beard identify
this mask as representing a Fon or
title-holder, and as such, it is a symbol
of authority. It was probably a part of a
lineage mask group. The over-emphasis
of the profile was a unique sculptural
style of Bafum, Fungom and Esu
kingdoms.

38
Male Mask
Western Grassfields: probably
  northwestern perimeter
wood
35 cm high
19th Century

This mask may be *Mabu,* the regulatory society's lictor mask, or it may
be the leader mask of a lineage mask
group.

39
Male Mask
Western Grassfields: unspecified
wood with kaolin
36 cm high
19th Century

Mask of a lineage mask group.

40
*Male Mask
Western Grassfields: unspecified
wood, kaolin, traces of camwood
 powder
39 cm high
20th Century

This mask displays the typical bi-tufted
prestige cap associated with Fonship
and title-holders, thus symbolizing the
established hierarchic social order. The
mask often dances with a flywhisk and
a traditional vestment of royal cloth.

41
Male Mask
Western Grassfields: northwestern
 perimeter: Bafum or Fungom
 kingdoms
wood
34 cm high
19th Century

The prestige cap identifies this mask as
representative of a Fon or title-holder; it
would have been a part of a lineage
mask group.

42
Female Mask
Western Grassfields: unspecified
wood with kaolin
36 cm high
19th to 20th Century

Ngoin usually follows the leader mask
in the dance sequence which includes
several *Ngoin* masks to complement
the male human masks.

Female mask, *Ngoin,* of a lineage mask
group at a commemorative death
celebration in the kingdom of Oku.
T.N. 1974

43
*Female Mask
Western Grassfields: unspecified
wood with kaolin and traces of
    camwood powder
31 cm high
20th Century

This typical female mask, *Ngoin*, wears
the distinct headdress of royal titled
wives and symbolizes the role of women
as complementary to men. The complete traditional vestment consists of a
garment of blue and white royal cloth
and a flywhisk. The mask dances in
short contained steps appropriate to
her noble image.

44
Female Mask
Western Grassfields: possibly Bafut
    kingdom
wood, kaolin, traces of camwood
    powder
45 cm high
19th Century

The elliptic hairdress on this *Ngoin*
mask is realistically represented as hair
and shows the application of camwood
powder, a substance used to denote
cult status. Traditional custom pre-
scribed that titled royal wives shave
their heads at the death of their Fon
and wear an elliptic sign of camwood
powder daubed centrally on the head.

55

45
Male Mask
Western Grassfields: unspecified
wood with kaolin
46 cm high
19th to 20th Century

The headdress of this mask shows
the blending of frog and spider icons,
referents to the important values of fertility and ancestral wisdom, making this
mask a demonstrative visual symbol.

46
Male Mask
Western Grassfields: unspecified
wood with kaolin
42 cm high
19th to 20th Century

This mask and the preceding example
originate from the same sculptor or
atelier. The same icons are present, yet
augmented by a lizard perching atop
the headdress.

47
Male Mask
Western Grassfields: unspecified
wood with traces of kaolin and
  camwood powder
37 cm high
19th to 20th Century

This mask represents the leader of a
lineage mask group. Ownership of
these mask groups is licensed by the
Fon and by Kwifoyn for a fee and con-
stitutes another acquisition of prestige
articles. Kwifoyn oversees the composi-

tion of mask types in such a group and
approves their iconography. Once a
mask group is established, its owner is
obliged to maintain it unless formally
absolved from this obligation by
Kwifoyn.

48
Goat Mask
Western Grassfields: unspecified
wood
51 cm high
19th to 20th Century

This image is that of a goat characterized by the two knobs which are not
uncommonly configured to approximate the form of a typical prestige
cap. For comparison of form and iden-
tical iconic motif (see Memorial Figure
of a Royal Titled Wife with Child, p. 23.).
The goat mask is optional for any mask
group, and its representation is linked
to the fact that the goat is the most important sacrificial animal.

49
*Bird Mask
Western Grassfields: unspecified
wood with kaolin
59 cm high
20th Century

In comparison with the coherent and
consistent cultural metaphors extant for
the other referent animals, the symbolic
quality of the bird remains equivocal.
Fragments of evidence may construe it
as a symbol for social manhood.

50
*Elephant Mask
Western Grassfields: unspecified
wood with kaolin
55 cm high
20th Century

The elephant mask is rarely represented in lineage mask groups, under-
scoring its exclusive status as a royal
icon. When it does appear, it is only
second to the leader mask and is the
last to appear in the sequence. It also
dances staidly in accordance with its
elevated status.

51
Male Mask
Western Grassfields: Babanki style
wood
48 cm high
19th to 20th Century

This important mask type is commonly only represented once in a lineage mask group. The multiple male heads reinforce the symbolic representation of lineage strength.

The hand of a master sculptor is manifest in this perfect work illustrating the style of Babanki. In our (Western) perception Babanki style exemplifies the most pleasing of Grassfields mask styles. Here the typically full cheeks and massive forehead are evenly balanced and tempered to a degree of muted naturalism. Babanki style masks retain the imposing presence which characterizes Grassfields art, but are without its aggressively expressionistic quality. It is the ''prettiest'' style of the Grassfields.

59

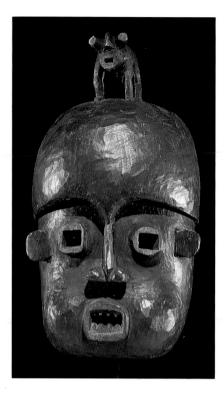

52
Human Face Mask with Quadruped
Western Forest: Widekum people
wood with accents of camwood powder
31.5 cm high
19th to 20th Century

53
Human Face Mask
Western Forest: Widekum people
wood, cowrie shells, residue of
   camwood powder
30 cm high
19th to 20th Century

These masks of the Widekum, who are
located in the Forest lowlands directly
west of the Grassfields escarpment, are
examples of a mask type used in the
men's secret societies of the Western
Forest groups. The style of these
masks shows affinity to that style prevailing among Western Forest cultures
in adjacent Nigeria rather than to the
style patterns of the Grassfields. The
small, open, protruding mouth and
analagous rendering of eyes, together
with the domed cranium are common
features of Forest sculpture along the
Cross River. These masks, alone in the
exhibition, were worn covering the
face, the open eye sockets providing
visibility for the bearer. Although their
village provenance cannot be specified
because of a lack of collecting information, they appear to have originated
from the hands of one sculptor.

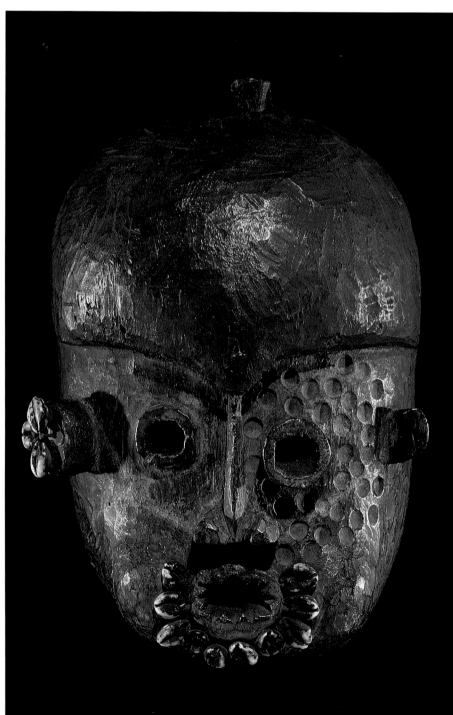

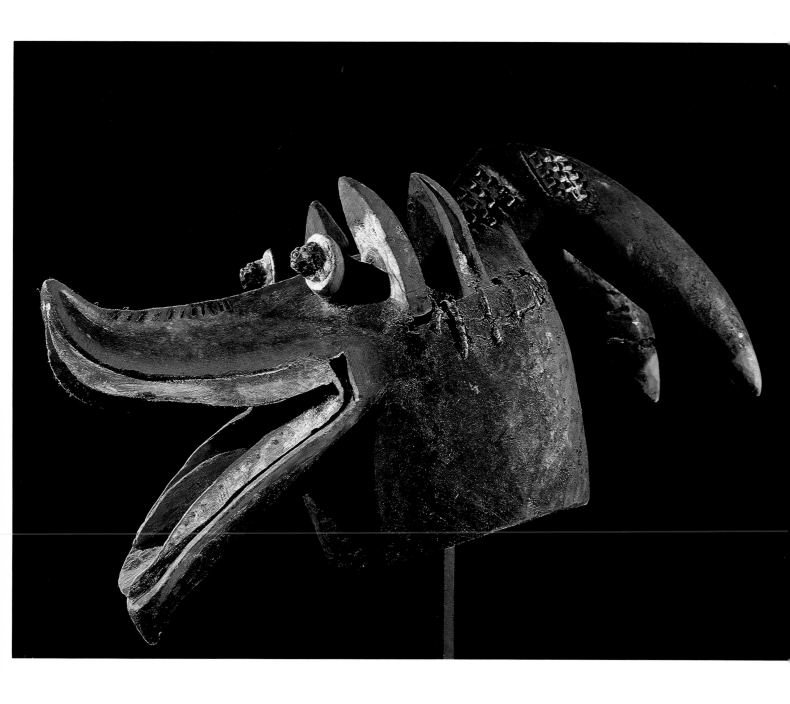

54
Zoomorphic Mask
Northern Plateau area: Mambila people
wood, charcoal, kaolin, camwood
  powder
25.5 cm high, 50 cm long
19th to 20th Century

A crow mask such as this is of secondary rank and accompanies the dog mask of the first rank. Masks appear at the biannual agricultural dances when they dance in a special dance ground in the center of the village. They can only be seen by men.

55
*Buffalo Mask
Western Grassfields: unspecified
wood, kaolin
65 cm high
20th Century

The buffalo was a large game animal
whose massive physique recommended
association with power. Its adoption as
a royal referent animal is manifest in
many focal works of Grassfields royal
art. Yet, the system of symbolic thought
supportive of the visual evidence is less
developed than in the case of the other
royal animals; leopard, elephant and
serpent. In the hierarchy of these royal
animal icons the buffalo appears to
occupy a lower rank. Buffalo masks
are represented by multiple examples
in Kwifoyn and lineage mask groups.

Lineage mask group dancing, featur-
ing Buffalo masks at a commemorative death celebration in the kingdom
of Oku.
T.N. 1974

56
Buffalo Mask
Western Grassfields: unspecified
wood with traces of kaolin
64 cm high
19th to 20th Century

57
Buffalo Mask
Western Grassfields: unspecified
wood with traces of kaolin
75 cm high
19th to 20th Century

63

58
**Mask, Conceptualized Male
Human Face**
Grassfields: Central Bamileke people
wood
89 cm high
19th to 20th Century

This mask belongs to a rare type, of which only three were known until the mid-1960's. The documented collecting dates of these three examples range from 1904 to 1925 and permit the reasonable assumption that the tradition of these masks dates at least to the later part of the 19th Century. Since the mid-1960's several additional examples of this mask type have come to light, including this one. After initial debate about their authenticity, circumspect scholarship not only affirmed the authenticity of some of these lately-found works, including this example, but it also refined the criteria for defining their authenticity as well as their area of provenance.

It now appears that these masks originated from several central Bamileke kingdoms, including Bafounda, Bamendjo, Batcham and Bandjoun. Bamendjo in particular is also known as the provenance for other spectacular mask types, notably the large male mask with crocodile headdress in P. Harter's collection and its pendant in the Field Museum (nr. 175595) as well as the most dramatic and sensitively rendered of buffalo masks (Northern: 1984, 168-169; and ex-collection Aga Khan, Sotheby, 1983: pl. 32).

Seen in this context, the post-1960 discovery of the unique mask type seen here confirms the remarkable conceptual vision of certain central Bamileke sculptors, without, however, giving us a clue to the time span of their work. This mask may date back to the 19th Century or it may be part of a continuing tradition in the 20th Century. Our knowledge of its meaning and use remain equally equivocal. But it is likely that it was one of those ''strong'' and most powerful masks reserved to play a prominent role in the Fon's installation in office.

65

59
Night Society Mask
Grassfields: Western Bamileke people
wood
48 cm long, 38 cm wide
19th Century

This Night Society mask is the feared emblem of the regulatory society on its nocturnal mission in "bad form." The awesome and fear-inspiring features of this mask give adequate expression to its aggressive policing function.

60
Male Mask
Grassfields: Bamileke people, possibly
    Bangangte kingdom
wood
31 cm high
19th Century

Among the Bamileke this mask is used
in the practice of witchcraft ordeals
which are conducted by an antiwitchcraft society.

61
Male Mask
Grassfields: Central Bamileke people
wood with kaolin
37 cm high
19th Century

This mask was probably also used by
an antiwitchcraft society. Witchcraft
was believed to be the cause of
diverse misfortunes, primarily illness
and death. Fear of witchcraft was
deep-seated and to practice witchcraft
was a severe infraction of the social
norm punishable by social alienation,
or in repeated instances by death.

Bangwa Royal Society Skin-Covered Helmet Mask

The Bangwa – the westernmost outpost of the Bamileke group – whose largest and best-known chiefdom is that of Fontem, are situated to the southwest of the Western Grassfields. Robert Brain, the anthropologist who conducted intensive fieldwork among the Bangwa during the 1960's, claims that their culture is basically "'grass-fields,' but enjoying the exuberant masquerades of the Cross River" (1972: 3). It appears that masquerades and cult objects have been trade items in this region for some considerable time.

In the Middle Cross River area of Nigeria, amongst the Ejagham, the tradition of covering carved wood masks with animal skin probably originated. The Bangwa have incorporated skin-covered cap and helmet masks into their masquerades, but Keith Nicklin says that "the trait of covering a mask with skin appears to have been adopted largely in relation to an established style, that is, superimposed onto pre-existing forms" (1979: 59).

This particular mask was probably made for use by the Bangwa "Royal Society" – a prestigious group which performs at funeral celebrations of members of the family of the Fon. According to Brain and Pollock (1971: 104) the style of the Royal Society helmet masks is "unique among Bangwa masks." Such masks may consist of one or more faces, often surmounted by smaller heads or figures. In general the faces either tend to have fleshy cheeks or depict prominent cheek-bones, with a small nose, protruding eyelids and a sharply down-curving mouth which is alternatively open or closed. Because of the upward slant of the eye some masks look superficially Oriental.

The piece in question is covered with very thin and somewhat flaky skin, which is probably animal bladder, though the Bangwa are known to use sheepskin for this purpose. The use of animal bladder and the skins of domesticated species contrasts with that of the more usual antelope and deer hide used amongst the Ejagham and related peoples. This probably represents the kind of technological modification that might be expected at the periphery of skin-covered mask distribution.

Jill Salmons

69

62
Helmet Mask
Grassfields: Bamileke people, Bangwa
wood with skin covering
40 cm high
19th to 20th Century

Mambila Masks

Living in hilly terrain, north of the Cameroon Grassfields, the Mambila are distinguished in their culture and art patterns from their neighbors of the Grassfields. Mambila mask sculpture is fairly consistently characterized by variations of a limited repertoire of zoomorphic images said to represent the crow, owl and dog, the Mambila hunter's valued companion. Their identification to date does not seem to provide sufficient cultural references to reveal the meaningful relationship between people and these animals.

64
Zoomorphic Mask
Northern Plateau area: Mambila people
wood, charcoal, kaolin,
    camwood powder
40 cm high, 43 cm long
19th to 20th Century

This mask also represents the dog image. The triumvirate of black, white and red colors — charcoal, kaolin and camwood powder — is a keynote feature of much of Mambila art. Camwood is a tree of the forest. It is a precious exchange commodity traded from the Western Forest area to the Grassfields whence the Mambila are said to obtain it in turn at great expense.

63
Zoomorphic Mask
Northern Plateau area: Mambila people
wood, charcoal, kaolin, camwood
    powder
16.5 cm high, 38 cm long
19th to 20th Century

Although of animal form, said to represent the dog, these masks are also of a rank requiring the use of other secondary masks during the biannual seasonal dances for men.

65
Zoomorphic Mask
Northern Plateau area: Mambila people
wood, charcoal, kaolin,
  camwood powder
37 cm high, 56 cm long
19th to 20th Century

This mask represents the crow, said to
be a frequent protagonist in Mambila
folklore.

66
**Mask Representing a Human Face
with Animal Horns**
Northern Plateau area: Mambila people
wood
29 cm high
19th to 20th Century

Masked dances for men take place at
the conclusion of the planting and
harvest seasons. This type of helmet
mask is of an importance requiring the
attendance of other secondary masks,
typically in animal form.

72

67-77
Group of 11 Standing Human Figures
Upper Cross River region:
  Ejagham/Keaka people
wood

(Fig.68) 52 cm

(Fig.73) 38 cm

(Fig.67) 46 cm

(Fig.71) 39 cm

(Fig.74) 40 cm

(Fig.69) 49 cm

(Fig.76) 42 cm

(Fig.70) 39 cm

(Fig.75) 35.5 cm

(Fig.72) 37 cm

(Fig.77) 40.5 cm

Keaka Figures

For many years there has been some confusion amongst African art scholars concerning certain Cameroon figures sometimes attributed to the Keaka, an Eastern Ejagham group neighboring the Banyang, west of the Bangwa, and at other times to the Kaka, a Tikar related group residing in the Mbem area, south of the Mambila region.

The difficulty can in part be explained by the seemingly close geographical proximity of these groups and the similarity in names. Further confusion results from the fact that figures from both areas are abstract in form, and there is therefore a tendancy to designate to these regions unprovenienced and relatively abstract figures that do not conform to the Grassfields rubric. Due to paucity of field data it is not possible to attribute the figures illustrated unequivocally to the Keaka region, although there are sufficient stylistic similarities between the Franklin figures, documented Keaka pieces, and carvings of neighboring groups, to suggest that they may indeed emanate from the Keaka region.

The Keaka and Banyang, two closely related groups, live in the forest region of southwest Cameroon, south of the northernmost reaches of the Cross River. In precolonial times, this area was at the center of two main trade routes of both north to south, and east to west axes, the former connecting the Cameroon Grassfields with the coastal area, and the latter linking the Bangwa with the Ejagham to the west. The Keaka are said to have held the monopoly over important salt wells of the area from which they manufacture their main trade commodity. This trade was supplemented by the manufacture and sale of huge canoes made from nearby forest trees, which were floated down the Monaya and Cross Rivers to clients to the south and west. The Banyang contributed trade goods in the form of livestock and slaves. In return for these goods among the items traded were cult agencies, associations, and their accompanying masquerade paraphernalia. Although alliances were formed between Keaka villages for the protection of the salt springs against the incursions of the Mbo, their neighbors to the south, for the most part each village was strictly autonomous. Trade was extremely important for Keaka society and vestiges of traditional trading patterns continue to the present day. For example, the Keaka town of Mbakang retains some ties with the Qua, an Ejagham group living in Calabar, the main trading city on the mouth of the Cross River. At the death of an important Qua chief, Mbakang elders travel down to Calabar to pay their last respects, accompanied by masqueraders of the Nchebi society.

Alfred Mansfeld, a German colonial officer working in the area in the first decade of this century, collected the earliest ethnographic material from the Keaka. Most of his collection is now in Leningrad, but there are two pieces at the University of California, Los Angeles which are ex-White Collection. P. A. Talbot, Mansfeld's British counterpart on the Nigerian side of the border between the two countries, noted that after an unsuccessful uprising against the Germans in 1904 many Keaka had fled from Cameroon into Nigeria, leaving the area very sparsley populated. At that time the main male associations amongst the Ejagham on both sides of the border appear to have been Basinjom, a witchcraft detection society, and Ngbe, the Leopard society. However, many different societies existed at a local level, including Mkpe and Nchebi for Keaka men, and Ndem or Mboandem for women. The latter commemorated their dead members with effigies, formerly made of mud, but more recently made of cement.

It is not known whether any of the figures collected by Mansfeld, or those in this collection, were associated with the above societies, though if they were, it is possible that they were displayed in shrines relating to the traditional associations in question. However, a more specific suggestion is that these figures were connected with the control of witches, and may relate closely to the Njoo fetishes of the Bangwa (Brain 1980:219). In 1980 Hans-Joachim Koloss, conducting fieldwork in Kembong, one of the main Keaka towns, discovered that the nature healers use medicine, called *enok ateng* "fighting alone," which is localized in an anthropomorphic figural carving. The healer, commissioning a new figure from a local carver, asked for the statue to be able to stand without help and dictated the following instructions: "...it must be straight and have natural proportions, and it must have eyes, and ears to be able to see and hear. It need not be beautiful: instead it should look fearsome," (Koloss 1985:90). In order to invoke the spirit, herbs were applied to the body of the carving and the blood from a sacrificed cock was dropped onto the body whilst the healer chanted, "God, give power to this figure because all power in life comes from you, let things be good and not bad..." (op cit:90).

Koloss does not illustrate the carving nor does he discuss whether male or female attributes are carved on the figure. It is interesting to note that little attempt has been made to provide sexual identification in the form of breasts or genitalia on the figures illustrated here. Two of the figures show male genitalia, however, and several of the figures have both a stylized beard and broad shoulders which presumably represent male characteristics. Three figures without beards have what are most likely rudimentary female genitalia.

Compared to the remarkable variety of mask forms used amongst the Ejagham, there is an unusual dearth of figural sculpture both in the literature and in the field today among the Keaka (Nicklin and Salmons:1984). Whilst this makes direct comparisons virtually impossible, certain stylistic similarities to art of neighboring groups can be drawn. For example, the powerful bent knee form of several of the carvings is somewhat reminiscent of figures depicted surmounting helmet masks in the Bokyi (Boki) group of the Ejagham (op cit:26). Also there are a number of Cross River bronze figures (Brincard 1982:47-51, pl. H19) whose stance could be compared to that of Fig. 67, whilst a strange zoomorphic bronze (op cit: pl. H16) has facial features that may relate to the face of Fig. 73. Several of the figures have what appears to be a rudimentary sagittal crest of a similar type to that found on mask forms amongst the Keaka and Bokyi (op cit: 36, 38, 39). This may represent a stylized version of the type of helmet previously worn by warriors in this region. The in-turning feet of Fig. 73 and Fig. 68 which appear to be a pair, can be compared to a similar rendition depicted on a Bangwa drum (Brain and Pollock:98). The face of Fig. 76 strongly resembles a skin covered mask seen in 1978 in Mbakang.

The varied figures in this group have some stylistic "memories" in common which may reflect their possible use. We have already noted that the carver, whilst working within certain cultural constraints, is given a relatively free hand to determine the final configuration of *enok atang* figures. It appears that as amongst other African groups, the actual appearance of a carving made for divining or healing purposes is not as important as its effectiveness as a repository for a spirit. This flexibility concerning form has allowed a number of disparate styles to develop in this area.

Referring to the Nigerian-Cameroon forest zone, Brain writes (1980:105) "Villages and village groups were autonomous and considered themselves free to make their own choice regarding political and religious and recreational associations. The open-mindedness extended to sculpture and the artist had a wider choice of forms than he would have had in a more homogeneous area. Trading and cultural contact in the forest possibly sharpened the imagination of local carvers." It is this "sharpened imagination" that may have provided us with this remarkable group.

Jill Salmons

75

Provisional Stylistic Comparison Chart

Western Grassfields

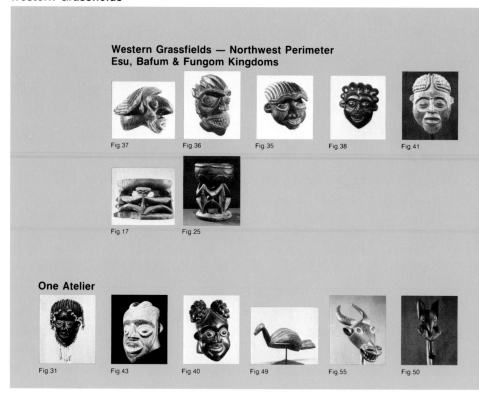

**Western Grassfields — Northwest Perimeter
Esu, Bafum & Fungom Kingdoms**

Fig.37   Fig.36   Fig.35   Fig.38   Fig.41

Fig.17   Fig.25

One Atelier

Fig.31   Fig.43   Fig.40   Fig.49   Fig.55   Fig.50

Western Grassfields Periphery

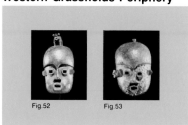

Fig.52   Fig.53

Upper Cross River Region — Ejagham/Keaka

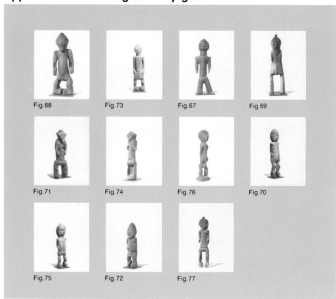

Fig.68   Fig.73   Fig.67   Fig.69

Fig.71   Fig.74   Fig.76   Fig.70

Fig.75   Fig.72   Fig.77

Bamileke

Specified

CENTRAL
Fig.58

WESTERN
Fig.59

CENTRAL
Fig.61

BANGANGTE
KINGDOM
Fig.60

BANGANGTE
KINGDOM
Fig.18

BAGAM KINGDOM
Fig.20

BAGAM KINGDOM
Fig.21

Bangwa

BANGWA-FONTEM
Fig.7   Fig.6

Fig.62

SOUTHWEST FOREST:MBO
Fig.3

All provenances except for the Bangwa pair are attributed.

Northern Grassfields Periphery — Mambila

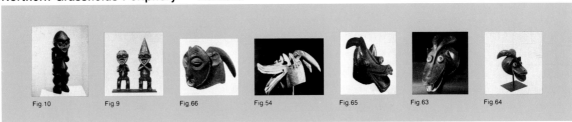

Fig.10 Fig.9 Fig.66 Fig.54 Fig.65 Fig.63 Fig.64

Specified

Unspecified General

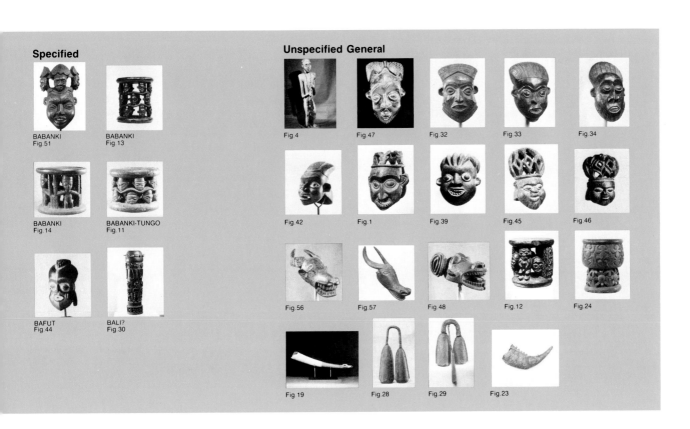

BABANKI
Fig.51

BABANKI
Fig.13

BABANKI
Fig.14

BABANKI-TUNGO
Fig.11

BAFUT
Fig.44

BALI?
Fig.30

Fig.4 Fig.47 Fig.32 Fig.33 Fig.34

Fig.42 Fig.1 Fig.39 Fig.45 Fig.46

Fig.56 Fig.57 Fig.48 Fig.12 Fig.24

Fig.19 Fig.28 Fig.29 Fig.23

Unspecified

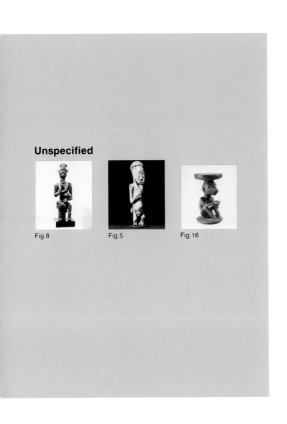

Fig.8 Fig.5 Fig.16

Bamum

Fig.15 Fig.22

BAMUM OR EASTERN BAMILEKE
Fig.26 Fig.27

Eastern Grassfields Periphery — Tikar

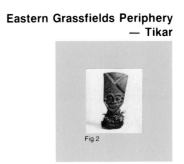

Fig.2

Bibliography

Brain, Robert and Adam Pollock, *Bangwa Funerary Sculpture,* (Toronto, 1971.)

Brain, Robert, *Bangwa Kinship and Marriage* (Cambridge, 1972.)

Brincard, Marie-Therese, ed., *The Art of Metal in Africa,* (New York, 1982.)

Conrau, Gustav, *Im Lande der Bangwa,* (Kolonialblatt, XII, 1899.)

Fagg, William, *African Sculpture* (Washington D.C., 1969.)

Gebauer, Paul, *Art of Cameroon,* (Portland, 1979.)

Koloss, Hans-Joachim, *Njom among the Ejagham* in African Arts, (Los Angeles, November 1984, vol. 18, no. 1.)

Koloss, Hans-Joachim, *Basinjom among the Ejagham* in African Arts, (Los Angeles, February 1985, vol. 18, no. 2.)

Lecoq, Raymond, *Les Bamiléké,* (Paris, 1953.)

Mansfeld, Alfred, *Urwald Dokumente,* (Berlin, 1908.)

Nicklin, Keith, *Skin Covered Masks of Cameroon* in African Arts, (Los Angeles, February 1979, vol. XII, no. 2.)

Nicklin, Keith and Jill Salmons, *Cross River Art Styles* in African Arts, (Los Angeles, November 1984, vol. 18, no. 1.)

Northern, Tamara, *Royal Art of Cameroon,* (Hanover, 1973.)

Northern, Tamara, *The Art of the Cameroon,* (Washington D.C., 1984.)

Olderogge, D., *L'Art de Afrique Noire,* (Prague, 1969.)

Ruel, Malcolm, *Leopards and Leaders, Constitutional Politics Among a Cross River People,* (London, 1969.)

Schwartz, Nancy Beth, *Mambila Art and Material Culture,* (Milwaukee, 1976.)

Talbot, P.A., *In the Shadow of the Bush,* (London, 1969.)

Talbot, P.A., *The People of Southern Nigeria,* Vol. II, (London, 1969.)

von Sydow, Eckart, *Handbuch der Westafrikanischen Plastik,* (Berlin, 1930.)

DATE DUE